---Law of Attraction Workbook---

How to Raise Your Vibration in 5 Days or Less to Start Manifesting Your Dream Reality

---

Ready to Manifest with Joy and Ease?

By Elena G.Rivers

Copyright Elena G.Rivers © 2019, 2022

Copyright Elena G.Rivers © 2017, 2022 - All rights reserved.

Legal Notice:

This book is copyright protected. It for personal use only.

Disclaimer Notice:

Please note the information contained in this document is for educational and entertainment purposes only. Every attempt has been made to provide accurate, up to date and completely reliable information. No warranties of any kind are expressed or implied.

Readers acknowledge that the author is not engaging in the rendering of legal, financial, medical or professional advice. By reading this eBook, the reader agrees that under no circumstances are we responsible for any losses, direct or indirect, which are incurred as a result of the use of information contained within this document, including, but not limited to, errors, omissions, or inaccuracies.

We recommend you always talk to a licensed professional in regard to any medical, financial, legal or mental health concerns.

Contents

Introduction 10

Day 1-Life's Energy and its Manifestations 14

Day 2-The Nature of Thought 23

    Focus of attention 24

    Our Relationship with Thought 25

    Positive Thinking 27

    Transcendence 28

Day 3-Meditation 35

    Expectations 35

    Aligned Meditation Method 37

Day 4-Resistance and Acceptance 44

Day 5-50Courage to be Yourself 50

Conclusion 55

Resources: FREE MP3- Limiting Beliefs Destroyer 59

Money Vibration Quiz 61

Free Reading - What's Blocking Your Manifestations? 63

Introduction

For those of us who seek out spiritual teachings or self-empowerment techniques, I have a question for you.

Why do we do it? Why do we look for these teachings and practices? In fact, why do we pursue anything in life?

Regardless of how we may respond to these questions, the fundamental reason for seeking anything is because **we believe that we will become happier** if we achieve its attainment.

Allow me to present another question to you:

-What is happiness? Besides being an emotion or the experience of feeling good, what is it?

-Where does it come from? How can we hope to achieve happiness if we do not know its nature?

The problem that most of us encounter in trying to become happier is that we **treat happiness as if it was a commodity**.

We may say thing to ourselves like:

- "When I find the right relationship, then I will be happy."
- **"When I make enough money, then I will be happy."**
- "How can I be happy given what I have experienced in the past?"
- **"How can I be happy living this way?"**

Regardless of what we tell ourselves, most of us have made the happiness that we desire **contingent upon us doing or accomplishing something**.

Even those who are spiritually-minded can fall into this trap.

An example would be the Law of Attraction.

Many people **become frustrated** that they are unable to manifest their desires because they have fallen for the same kind of thinking.

They start doubting themselves because their experiences did not match their expectations.

This workbook is about delving deeper than the pursuit of happiness. Instead, it is about **developing**

an understanding of the source that affects every aspect of our being.

The aspect that I am referring to is **our vibrational frequency**, also known as our life force. This book will give you a **five-day plan** to raise your vibrational frequency on a deeper level (we're talking about powerful mindset and energy shifts…) so that you can **spontaneously experience what you desire**, rather than trying/struggling to achieve it.

Now, let's get started on our vibration-raising exercises…

As I said…they all go deep in terms of shifting your mindset and energy so that you can FUSE yourself with your desires and manifest them with joy and ease, while having fun with the process (because it should be fun!)

Day 1-Life's Energy and its Manifestations

When I speak about "vibrations," I am referring to energy.

Everything that you experience, whether it is your thoughts, sensations, or feelings, is made of energy.

At the most fundamental level, all that exists is energy. At the most fundamental level, everything is one. You, this book that you are reading, and the object that you are sitting on are one in the same.

It is only in our current level of awareness that you and I appear to exist as separate entities from the rest of the world.

We cannot experience this energy in its purest form.

However, we can experience the expressions of it. Our thoughts, emotions, and feelings are a manifestation of this energy. Our physical bodies, which are also a manifestation of this energy, allow us to experience life.

Because of this, how we are feeling and the way we experience the world around us are directly proportional to the how **aligned** we are with the source of this energy, which often referred to as the universe, the greater consciousness, your higher self, or God.

What we call this source is irrelevant. **How our lives are aligned with this source**, though, is extremely relevant!

As stated earlier, our **physical bodies** allow us to experience life, both our inner world and the outer realm. The information that we gain from our experiences is expressed as thoughts.

Unlike feelings, which are a direct connection to **source energy**, our thoughts are our unique interpretations of our experiences. Our emotions are the tangible expressions of our thoughts.

In other words, if you are experiencing the feelings of love or happiness, it is because you are having thoughts of the same nature. If you are experiencing emotions of fear or anger, you are experiencing thoughts of the same kind.

It is important to note that the thoughts that you experience are NOT your thoughts.

You attract thoughts to you, which is a function of the Law of Attraction. To better understand this, we will take a look a theory referred to as the larger **consciousness system**.

The source of all that we experience is pure consciousness.

Pure consciousness is pure energy that is free of thought or any form of experience. The nature of pure consciousness is an infinite potentiality, meaning that it can express itself in innumerable ways. Our physical bodies, minds, and thoughts are just a few examples of the expressions of pure consciousness. What this means is that we are multi-dimensional beings in that we are both physical beings and pure consciousness simultaneously.

We are consciousness manifested in physical form. Having physical structure allows us to experience the world.

Information from our experiences, in the form of thought, informs pure consciousness, which in turn, creates new experiences or manifestations that are consistent with the knowledge that it has gained from us.

Every thought that has ever, or will ever, be experienced is an aspect of what we frequently refer to as the collective consciousness, also known as **the Akashi Record.**

What you experience as being "your thoughts" enters your experience by your tapping into the **collective consciousness**. There is one thought that is inherently yours, the thought that "I exist."

All other thoughts are energized by this one thought. The "I" thought energizes other thoughts by giving them its attention.

Our feelings are **our direct connection to source energy**, also known as pure consciousness.

When we get involved with our thoughts, we lose our alignment with source energy.

When we learn to trust our feelings, we experience alignment.

The level of our vibration is related to how aligned we are with source energy.

Exercise 1

1. Think of a specific time when you were sad, worried, or depressed. Try to experience that memory as thoroughly as possible. Try to remember what you were feeling or thinking at the time.

2. *As you step into that memory, place your attention on how you are feeling. Does your body feel heavy? Does your body feel hard or tight? Discover for yourself what is that you are experiencing when you revisit that memory.*

3. Now repeat this exercise, but this time, think of a specific time when you experienced the feeling of love, joy, happiness, or contentment. Experience that memory as thoroughly as possible. As you step back into that memory, what is your sense of well-being like? How does your body feel? Does it feel different from when you felt sad, worried, or depressed?

4. *Without any form of judgment, experience the difference between these two states of being. What created the difference in the way that you felt?*

The reason why your body and sense of being were experienced differently while reliving your memories is because **your vibration changed**. Most likely, your body and sense of wellbeing felt lighter and subtler when you relived your positive memories as compared to your painful memories.

The **frequency** of your vibration was higher while experiencing positive thoughts and was lowered when you suffered unpleasant thoughts. Your positive thoughts created **alignment** between you and source energy. You experienced feelings of heaviness as your vibration dropped; you lost your alignment with source energy.

Your feelings are your barometer to your relationships with your essential being, source energy.

Your relationship with your essential being is reflected by your feelings, and your emotions are reflective of your relationship that you have with thoughts.

Your relationship with your thoughts refers to the level of attention that you are giving them.

Day 1 Homework

Take time throughout your day to check in with yourself.

What is your experience of your body?

Does it feel soft and subtle or does it feel heavy and tight?

Do you experience tension in your body or does it feel relaxed?

Also, check in with the quality of your thoughts and emotions. Are they pleasant, neutral, or unpleasant?

Regardless of what you experience with your thoughts, emotions, and body, do not try to change them or judge them. Whatever you experience is, accept what is happening at that moment. The only purpose of today's practice is to be aware of what is happening with you.

Day 2-The Nature of Thought

As mentioned in Day 1, thoughts are bits of information that are generated through our interactions with experience. A child that touches a hot stove develops an instant meaning or interpretation of that experience. That interpretation is information, which we know as thought. Because our physical self is part of a more **extensive consciousness system**, that thought of the child, through **the Law of Attraction**, will attract similar thoughts, for example:

- "I need to be careful when I am around stoves."
- *"Stoves are not to be touched."*
- "I will never do that again."

When we give lots of attention to the thoughts that we attract, we create that which we refer to as **a belief**.

 As disturbing some of our thoughts may seem, no thought holds any power over you. Thoughts lack any inherent power.

All thoughts derive their power from the attention that we give them. Rather than letting our thoughts control us, we need to learn **to change our relationship with our thoughts**.

How we do this is based on the amount of attention we give them.

Focus of attention

The thoughts that we give our attention to will become energized; they will become real for us. How we experience life is determined by the thoughts that we hold.

Our thoughts **become filters** that shape our perceptions. If I hold a thought that people are driven **by self-interest**, I will be suspicious of all those I have interactions with.

Because our emotions are a reflection of our thoughts, our emotional being will be in alignment with our thoughts and perceptions.

By focusing our attention on our thoughts and emotions, we personalized them.

They become the determining factor of how we experience ourselves. Because we identify with our **mind and body**, we lose our alignment with source energy.

Every aspect of our life is influenced by where we focus our attention. Ultimately, the key to **raising our vibration** is to direct our focus on those things that feel right for us.

To know what feels right for us, we need to be in touch with our feelings. Honoring our emotions and focusing on that which supports our feelings is the fundamental principle for energizing our lives.

Our Relationship with Thought

There are three general types of relationship that we have with our thoughts: Unconscious, positive thinking, and transcendent.

The type of relationship that you experience is related to your level of awareness to the nature of your thoughts, particularly the thought known as "I."

Unconscious

The vast majority of humanity **has a strong identification with their thoughts**. In other words, their sense of self is based on the thoughts that they are having. They cannot distinguish between themselves and the thoughts that they hold. Examples of this would be a person who believes:

- "I am a good person."
- *"I am unworthy."*
- "I am a father," or "I am a mother."
- *"I failed."*
- "I am happy."
- *"I guess I will never be happy."*

This is just a short list. If you focus on any thought you have about yourself, it will contribute to the way that you experience yourself.

Positive Thinking

Compared to unconscious thinking, positive thinking is a <u>step higher in self-awareness.</u> This is because there is an awareness that positive thoughts are more beneficial than negative thoughts.

The advantage of positive thinking is that it will **bring you closer to alignment** if you sincerely believe what you are telling yourself.

The **disadvantage** of positive thinking is that it will work against you if it goes against how you feel. An example of this is when you are in a relationship with someone and then rush into marriage. In your heart, you may have some doubt about the other person.

However, your mind keeps making excuses about why you should go ahead with your plans.

Any time we go against our feelings; we **deny their message** to us. If we continue to do this, we become disassociated from them.

Positive thinking is only useful, in the long term, when what we are thinking resonate as being true for us.

Transcendence

Having a transcendent relationship with our thoughts requires active and ongoing practice. It also requires a willingness to let go of your most strongly held beliefs.

At this level, we no longer identify with any thought or belief that appears in our awareness.

This does not mean you do not have thoughts and beliefs; rather, you no longer cling to any of them.

At this level, **you are simply the observer of them**. You do not have to reach this level to raise your vibration.

However, if you experience this level of awareness, your life will be transformed at a level that few others will be able to understand.

The critical takeaway from Day 2 is that you want to focus on the thoughts that **make you feel good.**

If you are holding thoughts that do not make you feel good, you **are out of alignment** with source energy.

You not feeling good is a symptom of a lack of alignment.

The next two exercises on the following page will allow you to develop a **direct experience** with the nature of thought.

Exercise 2

Close your eyes and relax.

1. I want you to imagine a full moon. Make this image as vivid and real as possible and then let it go.
2. *Now I want you to imagine a black cat. Again, make it as real as possible and then let it go.*
3. Lastly, imagine a glass of water. Make this image as real as you can and then let it go.
4. *Now, open your eyes.*

The exercise that you just did offers some profound insights to how you can raise your vibration.

Let me explain. It is my guess that when you imagined the full moon, black cat, and glass of water, it had little or no impact on how you experienced yourself.

Imagining a full moon did not change how you saw yourself as a person.

Imagining a black cat did not increase or decrease your sense of self-worth. Imagining a glass of water did not make you anxious about the future or guilty about the past.

As stated before, **thoughts have no inherent power**. It is us who provide them with the attention that energizes them.

Our thoughts become meaningful to us because we **make them significant**, which is why your mental images of the three objects had no impact on you.

The nature of thought, be it the thought of a full moon or the loss of a loved one, are the same! It is us who cast meaning onto a thought.

If you want to **raise your vibration**, it is important to catch yourself when you are **giving your attention** to a thought that does not bring you happiness or well-being.

It is **the personalizing of our thoughts** that cause us to lose our alignment with source energy.

Exercise 3

1. Sit down and take a moment to relax.
2. *While you are feeling relaxed, look around at your surroundings. As you look around, notice the quality of your experience as you take in your surroundings. Rate your experience on a*

scale from 1-10, with one being totally boring and ten being enjoyable and relaxing.

3. *I want you to close your eyes and imagine that you are a traveler from another planet. You have come to Earth to learn about this planet. Because you are from another planet, you have absolutely no knowledge of life on Earth. You have no words to describe what you experience, nor do you have any memories to refer to. You are a blank slate as you experience this world.*

4. *Now, open your eyes and take another look around you. When you are done observing, rate your experience on a scale from 1-10. Do you notice any difference between your first and second observation? How was your experience of observing with "fresh eyes" different from your first observations?*

Day 2 Homework

As you go through your day, take time to do the exercises that most resonate with you from Day 2. The more you practice these exercises, the more that you will <u>increase your awareness</u> of your deeper nature.

Day 3-Meditation

Of all the practices to raise your vibration, meditation is one of **the most effective**.

The challenge is that meditation is often taught in ways that diminish its effectiveness.

Thus, its potential benefits are not realized.
The following are obstacles that will prevent you from getting the most out of meditation:

Expectations

Many people who try to meditate experience thoughts that are self-defeating like:

- "Am I doing this right?"
- *"Nothing is happening."*
- "This is boring."
- *"Why am I experiencing this?"*
- "This is a waste of time; I have more important things to do."
- *"This is too hard."*

The above examples are examples of unconscious thinking. In other words, we have allowed ourselves to identify with our thoughts.

The purpose of meditation is to learn to create distance between you and your thoughts.

Meditation is most effective when we learn **to become an observer** of our experiences rather than a participant of it.

When we meditate, we should be like a scientist who is observing a rare bird.

A scientist does not want to interfere in any way with the bird. He or she just wants to observe it. Similarly, you want to observe anything that you experience.

To observe your experiences is to be aware of them. It is the awareness of your experiences that diminishes your sense of identification with them.

It is the weakening of **your self-identification** that raises your vibration.

Exercise 4 Aligned Meditation Method

The following **is a simple meditation** that will help you overcome the obstacles and reap their benefits.

Before explaining the meditation, here are two important guidelines:

1. Do not have any expectations of what you should experience or what you should not experience.
2. **Fully accept** anything that you experience. This means that you are not to judge, analyze, resist, or try to change anything that you experience.
3. Since our thoughts create the biggest obstacle to **raising our vibration,** strive to offer complete acceptance of any thought that you may experience.

Now for the meditation:

1. Sit down in a place that is comfortable. It does not matter if you choose to sit in a chair or on a pillow. The important thing is that you are comfortable.

2. *Close your eyes and breathe normally. Do not make any effort or try to make anything happen. Whatever you experience, allow it to happen.*
3. Now place your attention on your breath. Notice the sensations that you experience as the air travels in and out of your body.
4. *If you find yourself getting distracted by thought, simply accept that this has occurred and return your attention back to your breath. Do this regardless of how many times you become distracted.*
5. When you feel comfortable that you can maintain the focus of your awareness on your breath for a period of time (the length of time will vary from person to person), allow your attention to be carried wherever it wants to go; do not try to guide it.
6. *Allow yourself to be aware of whatever experience that you may encounter. Notice your thoughts, your feelings, your perceptions, and the sensations of the body. Whatever you experience, allow yourself to experience it with complete acceptance,*

including any negative thoughts or sensations that you may experience.

7. Notice that you are the one that is aware of all of your experiences. Everything that you experience is constantly in flux, changing from moment to moment.
8. *There is no thought, perception, sensation, or feeling that does not change in its quality. Thoughts, sensations, feelings, and perceptions all change in their intensity. Even an uncomfortable feeling will vary in its intensity, while other experiences appear and fade from existence. Allow yourself to observe these changes.*
9. Notice that despite the fact that your experiences are constantly changing, there is one thing that does not change. That thing is your awareness of experience.
10. *Whatever is that you experience, there is an awareness of it. The essence of who you are is this awareness. You are not your thoughts, your perceptions, feelings, or sensations. Who you are is the recognition of them.*

11. The more you practice this meditation, the more comfortable and efficient you will be in losing your identification with your mental phenomena.

The previous meditation exercise is a great way to learn to reduce your identification with your thoughts.

The reason the practice of meditation is so effective in reducing our identification with our thoughts is that it is direct.

You experience for yourself that you are the observer of thought instead of identifying with it.

There are other ways to reduce your identification with thought that is indirect and take more time and effort.

I bring this up only because I realize that not everyone is open to meditation. **These alternative methods** can be found in all of the great religions and even in the ethics that we were taught as children.

Here are a few examples:

- Do not judge.
- *Treat everyone with respect.*
- Treat others as you would yourself.
- *Love your neighbor.*
- Give more than you take.

What all of these examples have in common is that they cause us to focus our **attention on the positive aspects of others**. When we focus on the positive aspects of others, we remove our attention from us.

Removing our attention from ourselves **reduces our personal identification** to our thoughts, which also will cause your vibration to rise.

Day 3 Homework

-The exercise that you did for Day 3 is your homework for today. If you are able to, I would recommend repeating this exercise a second time today.

Mediation takes practice, and this exercise was just to get you started. I recommend that you do this exercise daily.

Meditate as long as you are able to, even if it is only a few minutes. Try to extend the time that you meditate each day.

Day 4-Resistance and Acceptance

One of the characteristics of unconscious thinking is **resistance**.

Our daily lives are filled with instances where we create resistance within ourselves.

Here is a short list of examples of how we create resistance:

- We **deny** or resist experiencing certain thoughts, feelings, or emotions.
- *We agree to do things that we do not feel like doing out of concern for what others may think.*
- We do not do what we feel like doing because we feel that we are not **worthy**, that it would be irresponsible, or because we are concerned about what other people would think.
- ***We do things that we do not enjoy*** *because we believe that we do not have a choice. An example of this would be working*

at a job that we do not enjoy or staying in a relationship that we find **unfulfilling**.

Remember that denying our feelings is what causes us to get out of alignment with our essential nature.

We are so used to creating resistance within ourselves because that is how we have been socialized. We have grown up with messages such as:

- Don't be selfish.
- *Don't put yourself first.*
- Don't think that way.
- *You should not feel that way.*
- You need to be responsible.
- *I don't care how you feel, just do it.*

Learning to **release the resistance** that you experience is the most powerful way for **increasing your vibration**.

Exercise 5

This exercise is to release the resistance that you hold in your body. Do the following:

1. Sit down and relax as though you were getting ready to meditate.
2. *Next, I want you to focus on your body and notice the messages that you are getting from it.*
3. When you get a message from your body, I want you to honor it.
4. *Whatever message that your body gives you, I want you to honor it by allowing it to happen.*
5. Let your body move the way it wants to. Spend as much time as you desire to do this exercise.

Exercise 6

The One-Day Challenge

This next exercise is difficult for most people, but it is very powerful. I want you to spend one day where you do not do anything that you do not want to do.

This means that if someone asks you to do something that you do not want to do, you will not do it. If you feel like there is something that you should be doing, but you do not want to do it, then you will not do it.

Obviously, there are certain things that we do not want to do, but we need to do them. Not many people want to do their taxes, but we have to. When you encounter such a situation, do the following:

1. Think of all the benefits that you will gain by doing the task until your resistance lowers.
2. *Find ways to make the task more enjoyable until your resistance lowers. For example, host an income tax party where you invite friends over so that you can do them together.*
3. If the previous suggestions do not work, wait until you can accept the situation for what it is and are willing to do the task.

It is important to understand that this exercise has nothing to do with the task itself. It is **about learning to change your perception of the task**. If you are unable to do this exercise for a full day, start off by doing it for shorter periods of time. Build up your ability until you can do it for a full day.

Day 4 Homework

Practice Exercise 6 daily for durations of time that work for you until you can go for a full day.

Day 5-Courage to be Yourself

The ultimate purpose of spiritual pursuits is to get to know the truth of who you are. Because of this, it could be said that it is the purpose of spiritual practice is to develop **the courage to be yourself**.

It takes courage to lead your life in a manner that resonates with your truth, rather than to live your life based on the **expectations of society**, your culture, or your family.

It takes courage to stand up to the resistance that you will face from others. Most people unquestionably accept the expectations that they have been socialized to.

As mentioned before, **your thoughts are not your own**. They are the part of the collective consciousness that each one of us is tapping into. By being true to yourself, in the way that you conduct your life, you will be attracting those thoughts that are consistent with your truth.

Exercise 7

The purpose of the information and exercises that you have read so far in this book was to **increase your self-awareness to your vibrational level.**

Your vibrational level is ultimately determined by what you're focusing your attention on.

To master your ability to **direct your attention** is to master your ability to raise your vibration.

Your ability to master your vibration will allow you to **master the Law of Attraction**. The following exercise incorporates the key elements from the previous exercises and will enhance your ability to **guide your attention.**

1. Sit down and relax by focusing on your breath. You may close your eyes if you wish to.
2. *Be aware of the thoughts, feelings, and emotions that you are experiencing. This can easily be done by asking this question: "Is what am I experiencing comfortable, neutral, or uncomfortable?"*
3. If you are not comfortable with what you're experiencing, place your attention on that

which makes your experience comfort. The best way to do this to ask yourself, "What can I focus on or think about that would give me a greater sense of peace?"

4. *The next step is to listen to your feelings. Unlike your thoughts and emotions, you can trust your feelings. We need to be aware of what our thoughts and emotions are telling us. However, we want to go with our feelings.*
5. Take some form of action that is consistent with what your feelings are telling you. To live our life in a way that is true to our heart is to honor our feelings.

At first, you will have to consciously ask yourself these questions. If you continuously practice this exercise, your mind will eventually ask these questions automatically for you.

The mind communicates its messages to you by thought.

The body communicates through the emotions and sensations that we experience.

Your essential being communicates through the feelings that you experience.

We want to be aware of the messages that our mind and body are giving us without resisting, avoiding, or trying to change them. We want to listen to our feelings and let them guide us.

Homework Day Five

-During your day, apply **Exercise 7 (from page 51)**

Conclusion

This five-day plan was intended to introduce you to different ways of raising your vibration. Just as in wine tasting, it offered you a sampling of different techniques to try out. If you follow the five-day plan as instructed, you will experience a shift in your awareness, therefore permanently raising your vibration.

The more **you increase your awareness**, the more you will increase your vibration and **become realigned with source consciousness**. Don't treat the last five days as the end; it is just the beginning.

Your final assignment is to choose those exercises that resonated with you and practice them daily, even if it just a few minutes, until you experience the level of vibration that you desire.

To amplify what you've learned through this eBook, be sure to check out the following pages and the recommended resources created for you by other manifestation teachers who helped me on my LOA quest.

Until next time, wishing you all the best on your manifestation journey!

Love,

Elena G.Rivers

Your friend and guide in conscious manifesting

Bonus Resources from Other Manifestation Teachers

FREE MP3 Download - Limiting Beliefs Destroyer

What if there was one weird sound… based on the latest brain research…

That could radically change your life… By destroying the limiting beliefs that are holding you back right now? Would you want to know what it is?

And wouldn't you download it ASAP if it was 100% free?

Download the "Limiting Beliefs Destroyer" MP3 right HERE:

Think about it. EVERYONE struggles with limiting beliefs. It's part of the human condition. And those limiting beliefs are what's holding you back from experiencing and enjoying...

All the money, love, happiness, health, and freedom you deserve. When we came across this latest neurological research on the power of brainwave technology... we just had to get this one MP3 into your hands as fast as I could.

Download this 100% life-changing MP3 today:

www.loaforsuccess.com/free-audio

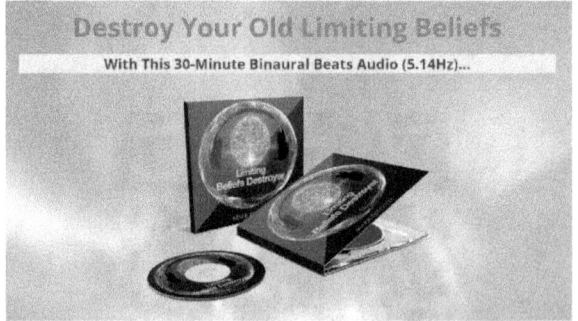

Money Vibration Quiz

Your Money Vibration is a good predictor how much money you have today. The HIGHER vibrational frequency you have, and it's a number, the higher manifestation power you have.

There are 3 LEVELS of money vibration:

Level 1 - You commonly say: "I'm drowning in debt" or 'I can't save a cent"

Level 2 - You commonly say: "I never seem to get ahead"

Level 3 - You would say: "I'm now ready to retire"

Take the Money Vibration quiz HERE:

Or visit:

www.loaforsuccess.com/vibration-free-test

As an added bonus, you will get 2-3 ideas on how to raise your money vibration to the next level!

To your unlimited abundance

Elena & Stephanie

Free Reading - What's Blocking Your Manifestations?

You already know that the law of attraction works. It is either bringing you closer to what you want or it repels you further away. The question is - do you know what is blocking you from attracting what you want?

International manifestation expert, Croix Sather has created a short manifestation quiz you can access here:

It will help you discover your manifestation block and break through!

It's fun and it's accurate ... and it will help you go from repelling what you want ... to attracting what you want.

Or, if you're already manifesting your desires, it will help you take your game to the next level!

Visit:

www.loaforsuccess.com/manifestation-reading

for your personalized manifestation reading.

This will only take a minute, but you will benefit for the rest of your life!

www.ingramcontent.com/pod-product-compliance
Lightning Source LLC
Chambersburg PA
CBHW072209100526
44589CB00015B/2442